IMAGES C

Slough
A Century of Change

Royal visit, June 1904. Their Majesties King Edward VII and Queen Alexandra drove through Slough, passing along Mackenzie Street, the High Street and Windsor Road on their way to Windsor Castle (The scene in this photograph follows the one on page 104).

IMAGES OF ENGLAND

Slough
A Century of Change

Peter Burgess and Judith Hunter

NONSUCH

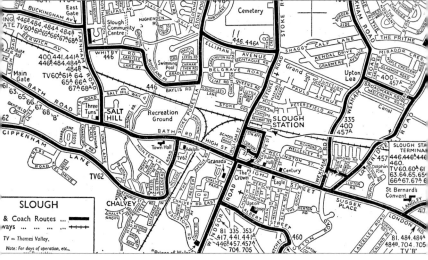

This 1963 map of Slough shows the centre before redevelopment, along with the London Transport and Thames Valley bus routes before deregulation in the 1980s.

First published 1999
This new pocket edition 2005
Images unchanged from first edition

Nonsuch Publishing Limited
The Mill, Brimscombe Port,
Stroud, Gloucestershire, GL5 2QG
www.nonsuch-publishing.com

British Library Cataloguing in Publication Data.
A catalogue record for this book is available from the British Library.

ISBN 1-84588-122-2

Typesetting and origination by Nonsuch Publishing Limited
Printed in Great Britain by Oaklands Book Services Limited

Contents

Picture Credits

The authors would like to thank the following people and organizations for use of their photographs. The pictures are listed by page number; 't' indicates the top picture and 'b' the bottom where there is more than one picture on a page.

Peter Aust: 122t, 122b.
Mrs Vi Ballinger: 11b, 14b, 16b, 19t, 26t, 26b, 38t, 39t, 53t, 54b, 66b, 67t, 69t, 73t, 74b, 77t, 79, 81t, 89b, 92t, 92b, 96t, 97t, 97b, 98t, 101b, 105b, 117t, 119t.
Michael Barrett: 72t.
Michael Bayley: 64b, 65t, 65b, 109t, 109b.
Terry Brown: 10t, 11t, 12t, 14t, 18b, 19b, 20t, 21t, 24t, 27t, 35b, 39b, 40b, 41, 51t, 51b, 52t, 56t, 61b, 81b, 82b, 86t, 86b, 90t, 90b, 91t, 91b, 93t, 93b, 96b, 104b, 107t, 107b, 108t, 108b, 111t, 113, 114t, 115b, 117b, 120t, 120b, 121t, 121b, 128t.
Buckinghamshire Record Office: 59.
Peter Burgess: 15t, 15b, 17t, 20b, 22, 27b, 30b, 34b, 35t, 37t, 38b, 42t, 43t, 50b, 54t, 58t, 61t, 63t, 66t, 67b, 68t, 68b, 69b, 70b, 71t, 71b, 72b, 76t, 76b, 77b, 78, 82t, 84t, 84b, 88t, 89t, 94t, 94b, 98b, 100b, 104t, 106t, 110t, 112t, 112b, 114b, 116t, 116b, 118b, 123t, 123b, 124t, 124b, 125t, 125b, 126, 128b.
Clive Currie: 106b.
Dunlop Ltd: 23.
Peter Faulkner: 42b, 48t, 48b.
Mrs Elinor Gates: 2.
Greville Creative Group: 46t, 46b, 47t, 47b, 119b.
Guildhall Library, Corporation of London: 25.
Judith Hunter: 24b, 28t, 29t, 29b, 30t, 45b, 52b, 53b, 55b, 56b, 58b, 62b, 64t.
Kidderminster Railway Museum: 37b.
Leicestershire Record Office: 57.
Pamela Marson: 9.
Ron Milton: 44b.
Royal Borough Museum Collection: 36, 60t, 63b, 85, 95.
Allan (Tom) Sawyer: 10b, 21b, 28b, 34t, 40t, 44t, 50t, 55t, 70t, 74t, 75t, 83t, 88b, 100t, 101t, 105t.
Slough Library: 46t, 46b, 47t, 47b, 75b, 115t, 118t, 119b.
Slough Museum: 62t, 72t, 73b, 103.
Slough Observer: 12b, 13, 16t, 17b, 18t, 32t, 33, 43b, 45t, 49t, 49b, 60b, 80, 83b, 87, 99, 102, 110b.
SmithKline Beecham: 31, 111, 127t, 127b.

Introduction

Five years ago I happened to visit a local stamp and postcard fair at Worcester, where I now live. With nothing special in mind, I casually asked one of the dealers whether he had any postcards of Slough, my childhood home town. To my surprise he produced four cards from his Buckinghamshire section. They became the start of my postcard collection and rekindled my love of Slough where I lived from 1937 to 1964.

I had a very happy childhood and I have vivid memories of Slough, of my home and schools, and of the High Street along which I walked four times every day during term time. Not surprisingly, my earliest memories belong to the war years when my family slept in a Morrison shelter in the living room of our house in Chandos Street. The shelter was little more than a steel cage about 3ft 6in high with a ½in thick steel top. After the war the top became the base for my new Hornby Dublo model railway, and I was very upset when the Council removed the shelter in 1949. Going to school one day during the war, I was surprised to see the road by the General Post Office was littered with strips of aluminium foil. It was not until several years later that I discovered that the foil had been dropped by enemy bombers as an anti radar-detection device. I remember the street party organized to celebrate the end of hostilities, but much more poignant is the memory of the anticipation and excitement of visiting Mann's bicycle and toy shop soon after it received its first post-war delivery of Dinky toys – and the even greater pleasure of owning a new Dinky toy aeroplane, painted green.

Around 1942, when I was still only five years old, I developed an interest in trains. Later, like many of my contemporaries I became a train spotter, spending many of my Saturdays and after-school hours at Slough station or on one of the many local railway bridges. My most cherished memory is seeing and 'copping' (recording the train number) a Bulldog – an Aberdare, a rare Great Western Railway engine – pulling a long goods train through Slough.

Slough was a very lively place during my teenage years as far as I was concerned. I played badminton and table tennis at the St Laurence Youth Club which met at the Herschel Institute. The building is now an American church. I went square-dancing at the Community Centre, and competed against other clubs. On Saturday evenings there was ballroom dancing at the 'Palais' (the Public Hall in the High Street) with Joe Daniels and his Hot Shots or at the Adelphi Ballroom with Gordon Rees and the Adelphians.

The highlight of every August was the Slough Holiday Carnival which was held at Agars Plough. The carnival was started soon after the Second World War and was organized by Slough Council. It was well supported by local societies and charities and provided people with an opportunity to enjoy themselves over two weeks without the expense of going away. The carnival had a full arena show twice a day always with spectacular acts from around the world. Between shows there were other events, such as open-air wrestling, and where else could one hear the best of Jack Jackson's Record Round-up virtually all day blaring out from the fairground? Tunes such as Frankie Lane's 'Mule Train', Kay Starr's 'Wheel of Fortune' and Guy Mitchell's 'She Wears Red Feathers' were as exciting to us as any of today's pop stars are to today's young people.

Exploring Slough again has given me enormous pleasure, whether it has been through the old photographs and my memories, or on foot with a camera. It has been a challenge to link memory and photograph, and to identify the buildings and scenes from earlier periods and locate them today. It has been fascinating to discover how much one did not notice in one's youth, but which is there to discover today. In this I have enjoyed working with Judith. Our memories complement each other's; I left Slough in 1964 and Judith arrived two years later.

I would be delighted to hear from any of my classmates at Slough Grammar School, 1949–1954, or Slough College of Further Education, 1954–1961.

Peter Burgess, March 1999

Acknowledgements

The authors would like to express their grateful thanks to everyone who has helped in the production of this book and in particular the following:

Peter Aust, Mrs Vi Ballinger, Michael Bayley, Tim Cole of the Slough and Windsor Express, Clive Currie, Jennifer and John Denyer, Elinor Gates, Frank Lauriello, Sue and Peter Morris, Alan (Tom) Sawyer, Jennifer Sym and Sam Young of the *Slough Observer*, Valerie Venn of SmithKline Beecham and the staff at the National Foundation for Education Research, Slough Library, Slough Museum, the Society of Licensed Victuallers and the other organizations and individuals who have so kindly allowed us to use their pictures.

We have made every effort to establish copyright and have obtained permission to reproduce where required. However, if we have inadvertently omitted to do so for any old postcard we offer our sincere apologies.

Peter Burgess and Judith Hunter

Slough High Street looking east from the Crown crossroads, c. 1905. Note the large bicycle wheel on the top of F. Parker's cycle and motor works; they also advertise motor cars for hire.

One

The Changing Face of the High Street

Slough High Street came into existence in the mid-nineteenth century in the decade after the Great Western Railway gave the impetus that transformed the hamlet of Slough into a small market town. But what survives from that period? Very little, perhaps only Park Place and part of Buckingham Place. Of the landmarks cherished in the memories of those that knew the High Street before the great changes of the 1960s and '70s – the Public Hall or Leopold Institute, the Post Office, and the Royal Nursery with its lovely wisteria – none remain. There is many a postcard that shows no building that can still be seen today. Instead we must search for features that can be traced from the older photographs to the newer, until at last the sequences of changing appearances can be followed.

Slough High Street in 1983. This photograph reminds us of how quickly we can forget. Every one of the shops has changed occupiers, some more than once. The buildings are an intriguing mixture of ages. In the distant centre is the Grapes (Sports Bar), probably built in the 1830s when the pub was first licensed. The plain style of Buckingham Place, seen on the left of the photograph, belongs to the 1840s when Slough was developing from a village to a town; these shops were amongst the first purpose-built stores, with shopkeepers, their families and shop assistants living above the shop. Today part of the building has been demolished and rebuilt as The Goose in Town. Adjacent is the late Victorian building with its two gables which are so distinctive on many old postcards. Next to that is the modern building which replaced the Crown Inn.

High Street, Slough.

High Street, Slough.

Above: The gas lamp at Crown Corner at the turn of the century. The lamp was quite a distinctive feature of Crown Corner, standing as it did in the centre of the road. Few of the buildings in this stretch of the High Street have survived, but note the Grapes public house on the extreme left.

Left: A very ornate new design for the Crown Corner lamp, *c.* 1930. The hoardings on the left shield the site of the demolished Red Lion, soon to be replaced by the Prudential Building.

Crown Corner, looking northwards, c. 1950. The familiar curve of the Prudential Building is on the right. In the centre is the lamp.

A new type of lamp, c. 1959. As well as the new lamp and enlarged traffic island, there are two high-level lamps which shone red or green according to whether or not there had recently been a fatal road accident. The lamps were installed as part of the Slough Road Safety Campaign. During 1951 six people were killed and 438 injured on the roads in Slough.

Crown Corner looking west, early in the twentieth century. The Cornish brothers were grocers and butchers. Their shop stood on the north west corner, more or less where the library stands today. Note that the façade which faces the High Street is Georgian, and clearly much later than the building behind.

Crown Corner looking west, 1963. Crown Corner has now taken on a modern appearance, with Foster's replacing Cornish's shop. Other buildings have also been demolished and this stretch of the High Street was soon to become a mere cul-de-sac.

An aerial view of Slough High Street taken in September 1963. Crown Corner can be seen in the top left; notice the staggered crossroads, but with no Wellington Street roundabout the tall buildings of Slough College are some distance from the main road. Mackenzie Street leads off to the right of the High Street.

The High Street in the early twentieth century. A horse and cart belonging to the GWR waits outside Lipton's grocery shop. Notice the royal warrant arms above the door of Headington's, family miller, at the corner of Mackenzie Street on the right.

The junction of Mackenzie Street and the High Street in the 1950s. At this date the road led directly to the station and then all places north via Station Approach and Stoke Road, according to the sign post.

The Reindeer Inn, before 1934. The inn with its superb hanging lamp was a picturesque sight from the mid-eighteenth century to 1934 when it was rebuilt. The new building was pulled down in 1967 to make way for an extension to Marks and Spencers. Notice the beer is supplied by Neville Reid's Brewery of Windsor. The distinctive façade of Headington's on the right-hand side of the road marks the Mackenzie Street junction.

High Street, looking east. The ornate lamp on the left links this photograph with the one above. The wide doorway adjacent is the entrance to the inn yard. The notice above welcomes cyclists. The solid building just beyond the inn is Blanchett's, part of which was later occupied by Suter's, now Allders.

The High Street, looking east in the 1960s. Before pedestrianization the High Street was often choked with traffic.

The High Street, c. 1930. The clock on the Leopold Institute was a High Street landmark for some three quarters of a century until the hall was demolished in 1972 to make way for the Queensmere development. On the opposite side of the road was a short stretch of one-storey buildings, one of which was Harding's butchers shop. The royal arms which denote that John Harding was a royal warrant holder gives the building its rather strange roofline in the photograph.

A middle stretch of the High Street, early twentieth century. On the extreme left is the post office, resplendent in pink and cream bricks, on the corner of Chandos Street. It was the first purpose-built post office in Slough. Opened in 1893, eighty years later it was just one of several buildings demolished to make way for the Queensmere development. Chandos Street was also lost in the same redevelopment; its name is now used for one of the Queensmere malls.

The same stretch of the High Street in the 1960s. This foreshortened view looking down on the street gives a distorted impression of its curvature. The town's prosperity is reflected in the number of shoppers; it gave rise to the High Street's nickname of 'The Golden Mile'.

The old post office in around 1971, not long before it was demolished. Today the site is occupied by the Virgin cinema.

The sorting room in the post office, *c.* 1905.

The High Street looking west, c. 1910. The post office in the middle distance locates the photograph. To the right are E. Rabbitt's, ironmonger, and W. Burningham's, tobacconist. On the other side of the road are the premises of Anderson and Duffield, ironmongers, C. Dix, draper and C. Dunsoon, greengrocer. Were either of the two ironmongers responsible for the wonderful ironwork of the hanging lamps in the High Street?

The High Street looking west. The tall building on the right hand side of the road is the Palace Cinema. It was opened in September 1921, the third to be opened in Slough. It was renamed the Century in 1949 and demolished ten years later to make way for Waitrose supermarket.

The High Street looking east, early in the twentieth century. The three 'exotic' buildings on the right with gables, pinnacles and decorative windows can still be seen today if one looks above the shop fronts. Notice the sandwich-board man.

The High Street in around 1920, looking west from Alpha Street, which is on the extreme left.

The eastern end of the High Street, 1930s. The one-story building on the left is Charles Turner's shop, the last reminder in the High Street of the Royal Nursery where Mrs Sinkins' pink and many species of roses were cultivated. On the right are Grove Parade and David Greig's grocery shop, both built in the 1930s.

The eastern Slough High Street, early 1930s. Victor's Café was also a sub-post office. The building on the right with the curved roof line was a garage.

High Street features. Today's High Street buildings are a mixture of styles and dates, from the 1840s to yesterday. Only too often when we hurry along the street we see only the shop fronts, but above these are sometimes quite grand buildings and interesting details in brick and ironwork, clues to the history of the High Street and aspirations of its occupiers.

Two

The Great Bath Road

Slough came into being because of the great medieval highway linking London and Bristol. For centuries it was known as the Bristol Road, until Bath became the great pleasure resort of the rich. During the coaching era Slough developed as an important thoroughfare village, served by at least four stagecoach inns. A mile to the west was Salt Hill, a smaller thoroughfare village. Its most important inn was the Windmill which was used by stagecoaches in the eighteenth century, but which became far too grand in the nineteenth century to bother with such customers. The coming of the railway brought an end to the coaching trade and few of the photographs reflect this 'romantic era'. Instead many older photographs show a quiet and empty Bath Road with so little traffic that children can play in the road. The development of Slough Trading Estate, the increase in the number of motor cars and the rapid growth of Slough changed all this. Factories, houses and shops lined the road where once there had been fields of corn.

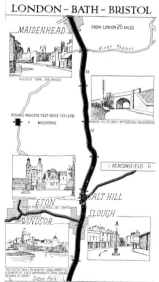

Dunlop's Map of the Bath Road, c. 1930. This pocket atlas follows the tradition of illustrated strip maps set by Matthew Paris in 1250 and John Ogilby in 1675. Notice the lamp in the Slough picture and the arrow indicating that traffic should keep to the left.

Colnbrook High Street and Market Square. Colnbrook lies at the eastern extremity of Slough and is now part of the borough. It was mentioned as early as 1106 as being on the road to London. In 1558 Princess Elizabeth slept at the George Inn for one night on her journey to Hampton Court, and in 1592 William Higgins, the innkeeper, was involved in a dispute with the butchers who set out their stalls in the market place in front of the inn to the hindrance of his customers.

Langley Broom in the 1970s. Now only a street name, Langley Broom was once a small area of heathland along the Bath Road. Here in 1722 a gibbet held the body of Benjamin Child, a highwayman who robbed the Bristol Mail.

A
NARRATIVE
OF THE
LIFE
OF
Mr. *Benjamin Childe.*

WHO WAS

Executed at *Langley-Broome*, in the County of *BUCKS*; and afterwards Hang'd in Chains, on *Friday*, the 9th of this Instant *March*, for Robbing the *Bristol Mail.*

Written by Himself while under Confinement.

To which is Added,

An ACCOUNT of his *Behaviour* while under Condemnation: With his last *Dying-Speech*, which he delivered to a Friend the Morning he was Executed.

LONDON:

Printed for T. PAYNE in *Pater-Noster-Row.* MDCCXXII.

The title page from the pamphlet printed when Benjamin Child was hanged. Such sensational confessions were produced for most occasions of this kind.

London Road in the 1920s. This tree-lined stretch of the Bath Road was part of Langley Marish Parish until 1930 when Slough's boundaries were extended to include the southern part of Langley.

Sussex Place, in the early 1900s. Although developed in the 1830s before Slough became a town, Sussex Place never became part of the High Street, its buildings remaining residential, not business premises.

The Bath Road through Salt Hill. The inn sign for the Swan, like many others in the early years of this century, has no pictorial representation of the name, though it proclaims its status as a hotel. No evidence has been found that the Swan was ever a coaching inn, though no doubt it catered for the passing trade and, like many another public house and inn, was proclaimed a hotel when this became fashionable in the latter years of the nineteenth century.

The Bath Road through Salt Hill. Not until the development of the Trading Estate did Slough expand and encompass Salt Hill. Today few people realize it was once a village. The inn sign in the middle distance is that of the Windmill Hotel. Notice the garage sign – but where are the cars?

Left: St Martin's church, Salt Hill, c. 1970. Salt Hill village lay at the boundary of the parishes of Upton cum Chalvey and Farnham Royal, and this small mission church was a joint venture by the churches of both. It was served by the clergy of Upton cum Chalvey until about 1950 when it was sold to a Pentecostal Church.

Below: A four-lane highway. Slough Trading Estate factories and a wide road built for motor traffic have transformed this stretch of the road which until the mid-twentieth century had been in the countryside. The land had been part of Cippenham Court Farm until taken over by the War Department when a Motor Depot was established during the First World War. After the war the depot was sold to become Slough Trading Estate.

SLOUGH TRADING ESTATE

L 6563

The archaeological hole, in the wall to the left of the photograph. For many years an iron-rimmed hole could be seen in the wall on the north side of this stretch of the Bath Road near Burnham Lane. The hole allowed hoses from steam wagons making their way along the road to take up water from the brook on the other side of the wall. The stream can no longer be seen, but Brook Path commemorates its existence.

A close-up of the hole.

Bath Road, Cippenham, in the 1950s. Unplanned ribbon development in the 1930s does not enhance this section of the road.

Ghosts on the Bath Road. According to the 1920s advertisement from which this drawing is taken, The Thames Valley Traction Company coaches slipped 'quietly through Slough, offering smooth effortless transport' every half hour.

Three

On the Move

Scheduled motorized public transport within Slough began in the early 1900s with GWR buses running to and from Slough station. They took passengers as far afield as Beaconsfield, Windsor and Hounslow. In 1931 most of the buses and routes were acquired by the Thames Valley Traction Company or the London General Omnibus Company, the forerunner of London Transport. Goods traffic was mostly handled by horse drawn vehicles until the mid-1920s, by which date motor lorries were becoming more available. The vehicle auction marts held by the Slough Trading Co. attracted buyers from far afield. A motorized lorry service was started by the GWR in 1925. It collected and delivered parcels and goods although a single horse-drawn wagon was still being used in Slough as late as the 1940s. It could be seen most days around lunchtime, the horse being tethered to a lamp-post in Chandos Street contentedly feeding from its nosebag while the driver partook of liquid refreshment round the corner.

Horlick's factory, c. 1936. The importance of the railway to the Horlick's site is well illustrated by this photograph. Like other works built close to the railway line, Horlick's had its own sidings.

The last steam train on the Slough Estates Railway. The Estate had its own GWR station, built originally for workers at the Motor Repair Depot.

Opposite: Fireman Jim Jarvis at work on the last steam train in 1973.

Slough railway station at the end of Mackenzie Street, in the 1920s. Built in 1882, this was Slough's second station. The first had a very strange design with both the up and down platforms being on the south side of the track.

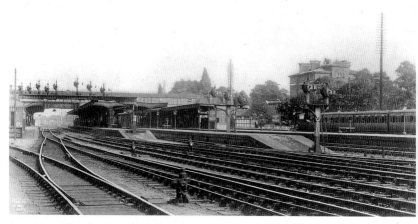

A view across Slough station. The tall building in the background is the Licensed Victuallers' School; Tesco now occupies the site.

Above: An express train leaving Slough station. The west-bound express is running on the relief, or slow, line; it is being pulled by a star-class locomotive.

Right: Flag day at Slough station, *c.* 1910.

No.—331 J.

GREAT WESTERN RAILWAY

IMPORTANT NOTICE.

OPENING OF INTERMEDIATE SIGNAL BOXES.

LONDON DIVISION.

ETON REGATTA, TUESDAY, JUNE 4TH.

The "Iver" and "Dolphin" intermediate Signal Boxes, situated between West Drayton and Langley and Langley and Slough, with their Distant and Home Signals controlling Trains running on the Main Lines, will be brought into use from 10.0 a.m. to 11.0 p.m.

The "Eton" intermediate Signal Box, situated between Slough and Windsor with its Distant and Home Signals, will also be brought into use for the first time between 10.0 a.m. and 11.0 p.m. on this date.

The special attention of all concerned is directed to this.

ALFRED HIGGINS,

PADDINGTON, 30th May, 1889.   *Divisional Superintendent.*

JUDD & Co., Limited, Printers, Farringdon Road and Doctors' Commons.

A GWR notice. Who would think of advertising the opening of a signal box today?

The Pembroke Coast Express passing a signal box to the east of Slough in 1959. The train left Paddington at 10.55 a.m., calling only at Newport, Cardiff and Swansea. It took only 128 minutes to cover the 133 miles to Newport at an average speed of 62.5mph.

View of an inspection coach in 1953. This view from the rear of the railway engineer's inspection coach looks towards Windsor at the Bath Road Junction signal box on the loop line from Slough West to the Windsor branch line.

Slough railway station before 1911. Horse-drawn cabs wait in line for passengers. These were the taxis of the era. They played a significant role in the development of Slough in the eleven years before the branch line to Windsor was constructed in 1849.

A GWR omnibus. This Milnes Daimler double-decker bus was on the Slough to Windsor route, judging by the advertisements. A bus service began in July 1904 to supplement the rail services. Buses left on the hour, every hour from nine o'clock in the morning to nine o'clock in the evening, taking fifteen minutes to complete the journey.

A London Transport Country bus outside the Royal Hotel. Route 460 carried passengers between Slough station and Staines Central railway station, via Datchet.

A double-decker bus in William Street, on route 446. In the 1950s the buses on this route ran from the Crown Hotel to the George public house in Farnham Road.

Slough High Street, 1920s. A single-decker bus is stopped outside the Leopold Institute.

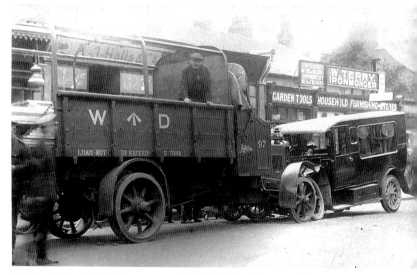

A mishap in Slough High Street opposite the Public Hall, c. 1918. How did it happen? The War Department lorry was a slow-moving vehicle and speed limits were in force.

Four

Inns, Pubs and Beerhouses

The history of Slough's inns and alehouses can be traced back to the sixteenth century when the village of Slough began to be an important stopping place on the Bristol and Bath road. At least four inns served stagecoach travellers during the coaching era. There were others in Salt Hill and Colnbrook, as well as inns catering for stage wagons, carriers and post-chaises (the hire cars of the coaching era). The coming of the railway and the introduction of beerhouses in 1830 brought about great changes, not least the loss of some of the inns and demotion of others to public house status. There was also a tremendous increase in the number of licensed premises. Today the majority of those older inns and public houses have been closed or their names changed.

Crown Corner, early in the twentieth century. The Crown Inn was the earliest in Slough, dating back at least to 1618, and for over 300 years it was the most important inn in Slough. It benefited from the coming of the railway, supplying cabs and post-chaises to meet the trains and offering accommodation to travellers. In contrast the Grapes was a beerhouse, acquiring its first licence in 1830.

"F. PEALLING" SERIES. THE BLACK BOY

Above: The Black Boy, which stood a little to the west of the Grapes, was a seventeenth-century alehouse, not an inn. It was closed in 1910, probably in response to new legislation which encouraged magistrates to refuse to renew the licences of 'surplus' and run-down public houses.

Left: The White Hart was another seventeenth-century coaching inn, though the façade seen in all the photographs belongs to the eighteenth century. In 1829 a fire in the stables meant that the Bath and Bristol stagecoach had to do without a change of horses. It was on the north side of the road, more or less on the western side of the present library site.

Above: The new Crown Inn. By the 1930s the attitude of the licensing magistrates had changed, and all over the country new, larger, 'improved' houses were replacing the old buildings. Breweries such as Courage were proud of what they achieved. The old inn was demolished in 1932; the new red brick building opened the following year.

Right: The Crown inn sign in 1963. The Crown was closed on 15 January 1966.

The Olde Reindeer Inn. A Reindeer Inn is recorded as early as 1618 and it may be the predecessor of the old inn shown in the photograph which was taken in the early twentieth century. Note the liquors sold, the provision of luncheon and teas, and the welcome given to cyclists.

The George, Colnbrook, in the 1890s. The George is probably the oldest inn in the area of present-day Slough. The building is sixteenth century with a late eighteenth-century façade. Princess Elizabeth (later Queen Elizabeth I) slept here for one night. It was a mail and stagecoach inn which became a hotel and then a public house after the construction of the railway line.

Above: The Grapes public house, 1961. The general appearance of the pub has not changed a great deal but, re-designed and refurbished, it is now known as the Sports Bar.

Right: The Grapes inn sign. Despite its name, the Grapes was originally a beer shop, which meant it was not licensed to sell wine. Perhaps it had an earlier name which was changed when it obtained a full licence.

THE GRAPES

45

The Eagle, 1940s. Like so many of Slough's public houses, the Eagle was opened as a beer shop in 1844. It stood at the corner of Park Street and the High Street. Notice the hanging lamps with the cockerel sign of the Courage Brewery.

The Golden Eagle, c. 1950. This was yet another beer shop; it opened in 1857. The hop leaf sign of Simond's Brewery of Reading is prominent. Next door to the pub was the Century Cinema.

The Floral Arms, 1930s. Set back from the High Street, the pub looks very much the same today as it did fifty years ago – except for the change of name and brewery. Today it is called the Pickled Newt. In 1930 the beer came from Harman's Brewery at Uxbridge.

The Pied Horse, 1940. The original Pied Horse was opened in 1704 against opposition from other victuallers in Slough. At that date Slough was only a cluster of houses around the Crown Corner crossroads and the site of the Pied Horse was some distance along the Bath Road. It was suggested that the site was a 'dangerous place for the harbouring of rogues and vagabonds'.

The Foresters Arms. Greater Slough had two pubs by this name: one in Chalvey, a beer shop originally called the Cricketers, and this one in Slough High Street just west of the White Hart. These photographs were taken in the early 1970s not long before it was demolished.

The Red Cow, Upton. The building is timber framed and some 300 or so years old, but the pub dates only from about 1860. Before that the Red Cow was on the south side of the road, from 1830. In 1851 Mary Mountford was the licensee. She ran a small dairy and this probably explains the pub name.

The opening of the new Langley Tavern, 1966. The mayor enjoys his pint. Today the pub is known as The Arkle.

The Brickmakers Arms, Stoke Road. Its name is a reminder of the brickmaking industry which flourished in this area for much of the nineteenth century. The name was changed to the Printer's Devil after the *Slough Observer* moved to Stoke Road.

Stoke Road looking north today. The pub is now known as the Printer and has been enlarged.

The Windsor Road looking south from Crown Corner. The photograph, taken in the early years of twentieth century, shows two 'inn signs', those of the Nags Head, a beerhouse opened in 1860, and that of the Leopold Restaurant – not a pub at all. Neither signs are pictorial, but then few were at this date. The Nags Head building still survives next door to the Sports Bar.

The Royal Oak was yet another beer shop which opened in 1844; it stood in the High Street not far from the Pied Horse. Note that its beer came from Ashby's Brewery at Staines.

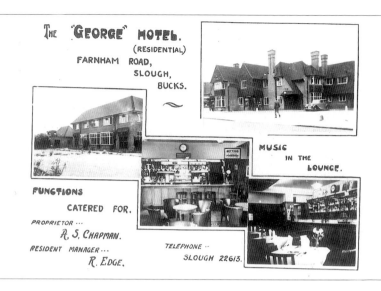

THE "GEORGE" HOTEL.

(RESIDENTIAL)

FARNHAM ROAD,
SLOUGH,
BUCKS.

MUSIC
IN THE
LOUNGE.

FUNCTIONS
CATERED FOR.

PROPRIETOR ...
A. S. CHAPMAN.

RESIDENT MANAGER ...
R. EDGE.

TELEPHONE --
SLOUGH 22613.

The George, Farnham Road. This was a large public house, built in the 1920s to serve the newly formed Trading Estate and this rapidly growing area of Slough. The George commemorated in the name must surely have been George V, but the sign that most people remember bore a very unflattering image of George VI, left.

The Kings Head and Barleycorn, Cippenham. For centuries there was no inn or alehouse in Cippenham village. Both of these and the Swan were opened as beerhouses in the mid-nineteenth century. In the 1920s residents had a choice of beers – Wethered's from Marlow, Simond's from Reading or Noak's from Windsor.

The Red Lion, Langley. This sixteenth-century timber-framed building may well have been built for Langley church as a church house (an early type of church hall), where the sale of Whitsun ale raised funds for the Church. The house remained the property of the Church long after it had become the Red Lion alehouse. The other two buildings in the photograph were formerly the De Pré School and the vicarage.

Botham's Windmill Inn at Salt Hill, before 1882. For about a hundred years the Windmill was one of the most prestigious inns on the Bath Road, serving the rich and noble, especially during the early nineteenth century when the Botham family were owners and innkeepers.

The Windmill Hotel, c. 1905. The old inn was burnt down in 1882, but long before this it had lost most of its coaching trade because of competition from the Great Western Railway. The new Windmill, built by Wethered's Brewery of Marlow, was a mere pub, not an inn – though it was called a hotel!

Above: The Windmill Hotel, Boxing Day 1911. The notice on the house next to the hotel advertises that there is accommodation for vehicles, be they horse and carriage or car. The message on the back of the postcard says that the writer had been installing a 'heating by hot water' system in the hotel in December 1912.

Right: A post-mill in terracotta. For more than half a century this delightful windmill sign has graced the roof of the pub. The original inn was most likely named after the post-mill which once stood in the arable field south of the Bath Road.

The Ostrich Inn, Colnbrook. This is often said to be the third oldest inn in England, a claim which can be traced back to a book on inns by Thomas Burke. Unfortunately documentary evidence has yet to prove it is much more than 400 years old.

An upstairs room in the Ostrich, 1970s. Why was the inn called The Ostrich? There is no easy answer, but it is not a unique name for a pub. These birds were not unknown in England even in the Middle Ages and they are mentioned in the Bible.

Five

Homes and Schools

Every town has its interesting old buildings, not least Slough – though it is too often dismissed as a new town which came into being with the coming of the railway or the Trading Estate! It did, of course, grow from a village to a small market town in the mid-nineteenth century, but its village origins lie in the far distant past, and within its modern bounds are, or have been, buildings of beauty, age and historic interest.

Almshouses at Langley. The picture is one of a pair of paintings by George Henton of the seventeenth-century almshouses at Langley built by Henry Seymour. It is a beautiful and accurate painting and almost certainly Henton took photographs to help him with the detail, for he did this for many of his paintings.

The Arbour Hill entrance to Upton Park in the snow. Upton Park was Slough's first residential estate. It was built for James Bedborough in the 1840s and '50s from designs by Benjamin Baud. The original plan included more than fifty elegant houses, a delightful communal park, stabling and three lodges. The park itself was renamed Herschel Park soon after it was bought by Slough Borough Council in 1949.

A mid-nineteenth century engraving of the park with its bridge, lake and wildfowl. Tucked away just south of the centre of Slough, Upton Park is a haven of quiet and seclusion. Its beautiful and unusual trees are now accessible for the public to enjoy.

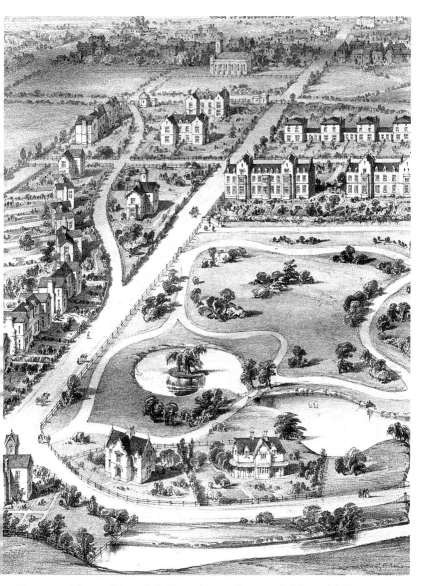

The proposed design of Upton Park. This is the central section of a lithograph by Benjamin Baud depicting the proposed new estate. Not all of the plan was executed.

Benjamin Baud

Architect

An engraving of Benjamin Baud. For more than a century it has been thought that Upton Park was designed by Joseph Paxton, but recent research would suggest that it was the work of Benjamin Baud, one of the architects who had worked under Jeffrey Wyattville at Windsor Castle.

Upton Park in the early 1960s. The pond, bridge and waterfowl would appear to have been part of the original design.

Right: Observatory House, Windsor Road. No book on the houses of Slough could omit a view of the house where William Herschel lived from 1786 to 1822 and where he built his 40ft telescope. The house was demolished in 1963 despite great opposition from local people. The picture is taken from a postcard posted in Slough on 3 September 1902 and is currently the oldest postmark recorded for a postcard of Slough by the *Picture Postcard* monthly magazine.

Below: Chalvey Park. Built in the 1840s in the no man's land between the growing town of Slough and the village of Chalvey, this residential development seems to have had a shadowy existence and is scarcely remembered.

Above: The rear view of Upton manor house, 1930s. Upton Court is Slough's only medieval domestic building. We know little of its early history, but it was certainly the manor house for Upton in 1605 when Thomas Duck, the tenant farmer, made his will.

Left: The restoration of Upton Court in 1987. A few years earlier, the house had been surveyed, revealing it to have been built in the early fourteenth century. It is thus one of the oldest houses in the county and now houses the offices of the *Slough Observer*.

The entrance to Upton Court. For many years the house was hidden from view at the end of the drive which was entered from Upton Court Road. Today it can be seen from the Datchet Road.

Henry Darvill, Lord of the Manor. Darvill had no connection with Upton Court, but he bought the lordship of the manor in 1852. He was a solicitor and town clerk at Windsor.

Above: Cippenham Court Farm from Cippenham Lane, 1970s. The photograph was taken not many years before the farm ceased to function and the buildings took on new uses. The stables in the middle distance have become the Long Barn public house.

Left: Mr and Mrs Whitworth at the door of Cippenham Court Farm, 1910. Whitworth was a tenant farmer in partnership with the Headingtons. The farm was one of the largest in South Buckinghamshire until it lost a large part of its land to the motor repair depot which was eventually to become Slough Trading Estate. The house was built around 1820; today it is used for offices. Mrs Whitworth's brother, Ernest Headington, lived above the shop in Slough High Street.

Sheep farming at Cippenham Court Farm, 1910. The sheep were bought in to be fattened for the London markets. They had probably been bought at the annual sheep fair at Slough market; on those occasions there were sheep pens over all the land between Horlick's, the railway and into Station Yard. In the background of the photograph can be seen about a dozen corn ricks.

Cippenham Court Farm, 1910. Two farm workers specialized in making hurdles for penning the sheep. The wood came from a coppice on the farm.

St Bernard's Convent. The house – Aldin House – was originally built for the Baroness Burdett-Coutts, a member of the great banking family. She never lived there and from 1869 to 1883 it was St Michael's School. In 1897 the house was bought by the Bernadines for a boarding school run in connection with their convent. Local day children were accepted from 1904.

St Joseph's School. This was also originally a private house. It became a day school for children of all denominations in 1906 and was amalgamated with St Bernard's in 1945. According to the brochure, the course of instruction comprised 'all the usual branches of a high class French and English education', but 'politeness and deportment' also received the 'greatest care and attention'.

Upton House School, c. 1910. This was a high-class, modern school for girls, to quote an advertisement of 1909. They were given a 'thorough education' by resident English and foreign mistresses and visiting masters.

Tower House. This impressive residence in Chalvey Park was a college throughout the 1930s.

The British Orphan Asylum. The building was originally the Royal Hotel, a grand establishment built for the Great Western Railway in around 1840. It had a waiting room for Queen Victoria. The hotel failed in 1852 after the construction of the branch line to Windsor resulted in a loss of trade. After a period of neglect, the building and adjoining land was purchased for the British Orphan Asylum by Edward Mackenzie.

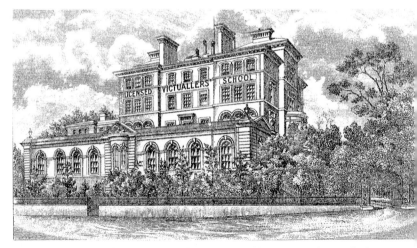

The Licensed Victuallers' School. The building was acquired by the Licensed Victuallers' Society in 1920. The old buildings were demolished in 1938 and a new school built, which was in turn demolished in the 1980s to make way for a Tesco supermarket.

Above: Baylis House. The house was built in around 1695 as a modest country seat. In 1829, however, it became a Roman Catholic school with an international reputation for excellence – not only in the education provided, but also through its association with the wine and spirit trade as it had connections with important wine producing families on the Continent.

Right: A label from a bottle of Baylis & Co. scotch whisky. Their shop was at 72 High Street.

Halidon House School for Girls. The school was founded as early as 1865 and for many years, under the headship of Miss Webb, it was one of the leading schools in Slough. It moved from its site in Mackenzie Street to Fulmer in 1948 and the building became the *Slough Observer* offices.

Form III at Halidon House School.

Above: Windsor House Preparatory School for Boys. This excellent school in the Windsor Road was run by Mr and Mrs Noding. It was closed in 1963.

Right: A pupil at Windsor House School. One of the authors, Peter Burgess, attended this school from 1942 to 1949. During air raids the whole school vacated the classrooms to take shelter in the kitchen and common room which were situated below ground level.

Eton Union Workhouse, before 1867. The workhouse was built as a result of the 1834 Poor Law Act to serve the nineteen parishes of south Buckinghamshire. Here were accommodated many of the destitute, orphans, unmarried mothers, tramps and the mentally ill. It was not meant to be a pleasant place, but the Eton Union was less awful than workhouses in some other unions. Mr C.P. Barrett, clerk to the Board of Guardians, is here seen talking to the master of the workhouse, Mr W.P. Philipps.

The workhouse became Upton Hospital in 1948. Today the building is part of the East Berkshire Health Service.

Slough Community Centre in the 1960s. The centre was opened in 1937, the first of its kind in England; it was hailed as a new experiment in social and recreational work. The old building was later demolished, to be replaced by a new centre of a very modern design.

A boxing match at Slough Community Centre in the late 1930s. The boys belonged to the Youth Centre Boys' Club.

The Paddington Green Children's Convalescent Home at the turn of the twentieth century. Sir Douglas Forsyth, who lived in Upton Court from 1883 to 1886, was instrumental in founding the home in Upton Road on a site now occupied by Dudley Court flats. The home later became known as the Paddington Green Children's Home.

Convalescent children at Paddington Green. The home took in twenty-four children from the Paddington Green Hospital in London. It was free to poor children 'without letters of recommendation'.

The Drill Hall and Club Room in Wellington Street. It was built in 1902 for the Oxfordshire and Buckinghamshire Light Infantry Battalion, C Company, by James Elliman, a great benefactor to Slough.

Home under canvas: Bucks Volunteers at camp before 1907.

Above: The Mere. The house was built in 1887 for Richard Bentley, a well-known London publisher, on land which had been originally part of Upton Park. Since 1964 the house has been the headquarters of the National Foundation for Educational Research.

Left: An intriguing extract from a book on the Mere garden.

Right: Advertisement for Nixey's. The Nixey family was established in Slough by 1851; Thomas Nixey was a wheelwright and blacksmith in the High Street, but there were several others with the same surname. In 1856 W.G. Nixey bought the old vicarage and built Springfield House in Upton. The popularity of his black lead gave rise to the nickname for the house – Black Lead Castle, a name by which the house is still known by local people, though its proper name is now Upton Towers.

Below: Upton Towers today.

A notice for Salt Hill Society. The society was founded in 1783 for 'the protection of persons and property from thieves, felons, highwaymen and footpads in the Hundreds of Burnham and Stoke', an area which covered the whole of south Buckinghamshire, including Slough. The society gave money awards to anyone who supplied information about damage to property which led to a prosecution. The society still meets today.

Six

Churches

There was no church in Slough during the centuries when it was a small village within the parish of Upton cum Chalvey. The parish church then was St Laurence's at Upton. St Mary's was built when Slough began to grow in the 1830s and for a while St Laurence's was allowed to fall into ruin. Within decades of Slough becoming a town, churches of various denominations were established in the town. Others have been built since and in 1894 the first new parish was carved out of the Parish of Upton cum Chalvey. With the expansion of Slough boundaries in 1930 and again later, other churches and parts of parishes were encompassed by the growing town.

The Roman Catholic church, 1911. For many years the local centre of Roman Catholic worship was Baylis House, a Roman Catholic school from 1830 to 1907. The church of Our Lady Immaculate and Saint Ethelbert was built in 1910. Perhaps the children outside were members of the Sunday school.

Slough parish church. This aerial view of St Mary's church was taken in 1964 from the Key West Building at Arbour Hill. The church was originally built in 1836, but has since been enlarged twice. The steeple was added in 1913.

PARISH CHURCH, SLOUGH.

Stones Royal Series

Above: St Mary's church, *c.* 1909. Without the steeple the church is a much less striking building.

Right: The war memorial in St Mary's churchyard. A.Y. Nutt, architect at Windsor Castle, was commissioned to design a war memorial for Slough to the dead of the First World War. Two designs were submitted; the one to stand outside Slough station was rejected.

War Memorial, Slough.

Above: The Congregational church in Church Street, Slough. The centre of Congregational worship moved from Chalvey to Slough in 1853 soon after the death of John Smith, grocer and church member who gave land for the Congregational church in Chalvey. When the foundation stone of the Slough church was laid 'worshippers came from far and near, on horseback and riding pillion or in farmers' carts'.

Left: The Baptist church, Windsor Road. This early twentieth-century photograph of the church shows how little the building has changed, but notice the 10mph speed limit post outside.

Right: The Tin Tabernacle. This was the nickname for the Stoke Road mission church which was built in 1885 and served this northern part of the town until St Paul's was built in 1906.

Below: The consecration of St George's church, Britwell, February 1961. The Britwell Estate was built in the 1950s by the London County Council. It only became part of the Borough of Slough after the local government re-organization of 1974. The church is now one of four making up the Parish of West Slough.

Above: St Laurence's church, Upton. This was the original parish church of Upton cum Chalvey – there was then no parish of Slough. St Laurence's was replaced by St Mary's in 1836, but by this date it was ruinous and without the intervention of John Pocock would have been demolished.

Left: The lich-gate at Upton church.

Opposite: St Laurence's. This engraving of the chancel of Upton church emphasises its Norman origin.

A Sunday school outing, early last century. The children of the Baptist church Sunday school are ready to set off on their outing. Like most other Sunday schools for miles around, they were almost certainly going to Burnham Beeches. Carts were loaned by local tradesmen, scrubbed out and fitted with benches for the occasion.

A Sunday school treat. Slough Free Church Sunday school and the Boys' Life Brigade parade on the occasion of the Sunday school treat. Captain A.W. Chambers and Lt J. Chambers lead the parade; they were joint founders.

Seven

Side Streets and Suburbs

For more than 500 years, from its origins in the Middle Ages to its development from a village to a small market town in the mid-nineteenth century, Slough consisted of little more than a cluster of buildings around Crown Corner and a few along the Bath Road. With the construction of the railway and the growth of the town came the laying out of streets north and south of the High Street. New side streets were also built in the ancient settlements of Chalvey, Cippenham and Langley, but it was the explosion of street and house building in the 1920s and 1930s which engulfed those villages and made them suburbs.

Windsor Road, looking south from Arbour Hill in 1964. The entrance to Herschel Park is on the left. Windsor Road has been an important highway since Windsor Castle was built in Norman times and there was a need for a road leading northwards to the next of the Conqueror's line of castles which encircled London.

Chalvey Road West looking west. Much in this 1930s view of the road can be seen today, including the church, the Foresters Arms public house (almost hidden by the lamp post) and the passageway on the right.

Chalvey Road East. An almost familiar view except for the absence of traffic and the advertisements.

King Edward Street, Chalvey. Little has changed in the appearance of this or any of the other Victorian streets of terraced houses – except for the vehicles. On the day of this photograph in 1910, or thereabouts, there was one milk cart where today the street would be lined with parked cars.

High Street, Chalvey, early this century. Of all the roads in Chalvey, this has changed the most. Today there are no shops and no old houses; its role as High Street has been taken over by Chalvey Road.

Ragstone Road, c. 1920. Houses were built along the road in the second half of the nineteenth century, but the road itself is very old. It is shown as a track on the earliest detailed map of the parish of 1773.

The Grove, Chalvey. The houses shown in the photograph appear to be mostly nineteenth century, but the Grove is also shown on the 1773 map; its curve follows the curve of the old village green.

Salt Hill Park. The Salt Hill Pleasure Grounds, to give the park its official name, were opened in 1907. The park, its gardens, tennis courts, restaurant (now the Barn Tandoori), children's playground and lodge were the gift of James Elliman.

Salt Hill Park in the 1930s.

Cippenham village, c. 1900. The Green was the heart of the old village, its houses mainly scattered around its edge. Here cattle once grazed, but since the end of last century it has been administered by a trust and it is now used for sports. It is the only ancient village green surviving within Slough's boundaries.

Lewin's Farm, Cippenham, 1940s. The name Lewin is found in records of Cippenham as early as the fifteenth century. The farmstead stood in Lower Cippenham Lane; it was demolished to make way for a housing estate in the 1970s.

Station Road, Cippenham. Without the caption this view of what is today a very busy main road would be very difficult to identify.

Cippenham Green.

Left: Montem Mound at Salt Hill. Its name is derived from an ancient ceremony – a rag day and fund raising occasion on which originally salt was given in exchange for money. The participants were boys from Eton College. The photograph was taken in 1892 by a member of the Herschel family.

Below: A modern picture of the Montem Mound. It is almost certainly a burial mound, Bronze Age or Saxon, and thus the oldest man-made feature in Slough.

Opposite: Getting ready for the Montem Ceremony at Eton College. The event was celebrated for some 400 years before it was abolished in 1847 because of the increase in unwelcome visitors from London.

MONTEM.

Day & Kaylo Lith to the Queen

Farnham Road looking north, 1930s. Behind this parade of shops lie housing estates built between the wars to accommodate the growing population which came to find work in Slough. Until 1930 when Slough's boundaries were extended, this area was part of Farnham Royal Parish.

Upton Road. With the construction of Yew Tree Road, Upton Road was made a cul-de-sac. But it is perhaps one of the most ancient roads in the town, anciently linking the village of Upton with the Bath Road.

Curzon Street looking east, c. 1905. This mainly residential street linking William Street and Mackenzie Street was one of the first roads to be demolished in the redevelopment of the town centre in the 1960s.

Mackenzie Street looking north, early twentieth century. Until the 1960s redevelopment Mackenzie Street linked the High Street and Station Approach.

William Street, at the turn of the twentieth century. Nothing remains today of these buildings and the names of the businesses – Cornish Fancy Goods, F. Smith, bootmaker, Robinson's hairdressers and Wheeler's coffee rooms – have long since been forgotten.

Stoke Road, looking towards the High Street from the railway bridge, early in the twentieth century. On the left is the North Star public house at the corner of Station Approach. When the trains stopped at Slough before the station was built, train tickets could be bought at the pub.

An aerial view of William Street, September 1963. William Street runs south to north across the page with the North Star Hotel on the corner of Station Approach near the bottom of the photograph. On the west side of William Street, from left to right, are the entrance to Slough College of Further Education, Goddard's furniture shop and Rabbitt's the ironmongers – a treasure trove for tools of all sizes. The car park next to the railway was the site of the original cattle market which closed in September 1961. The railway is curving southwards to Windsor.

A quiet view of the Uxbridge Road and Sussex Place junction.

A modern view of the same Uxbridge Road junction.

Wexham Road early in the twentieth century. Wexham Road was a country lane when Slough began to grow in the 1840s, but by the end of the century terraced houses had begun to line its southern end north of the Royal Nurseries.

The Myrke, Datchet Rd. Slough.

The Myrke, Datchet Road. The area is aptly named for 'myrke' means the boundary, and the name was originally applied to an area on the edge of the old parish of Upton cum Chalvey. Today it is the name of a road tucked away off the Datchet Road on the edge of Slough.

Windsor Road, 1964. This view is full of landmarks – the Horlick's chimney, Slough College tower blocks, the curve of the Prudential Building, and the solid block of the Granada Cinema with its licensed restaurant. In the far distance are the wooded slopes of the Chiltern dip slope. The waste ground (centre right) was the site of Observatory House.

Eight

Celebrations and Events

Slough is not an ancient borough. It began as a village and grew into a town with the coming of the railway. It was made an urban district in 1894. Slough's population grew rapidly in the 1920s and '30s with the development of the Slough Trading Estate and in 1930/31 its boundaries were expanded to take in parts of the several neighbouring parishes. In 1938 Slough was elevated from an urban district to a borough, receiving its charter from the King in September of that year.

Celebrations for the granting of Slough's Charter as a borough. Residents watch the Charter Parade.

Above: A Royal Visit in June 1904. Crowds cheer to see Edward VII and Queen Alexandra drive along Mackenzie Street, turning into the High Street en route to the Windsor Road.

Left: Local dignitaries make their way to the memorial service for Edward VII at St Mary's Church in 1910. Brooks Stores and the Reindeer Inn can be seen in the background.

Celebrations for the Coronation of George V and Queen Mary, July 1911. Slough High Street was gaily decorated for the event.

George V's coronation celebrations, 1911. Their Majesties drove through Slough on their way to Windsor Castle.

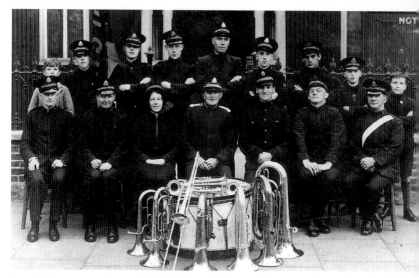

Slough Salvation Army band in 1936. Bandmaster Cresswell sits in the centre of the front row. The Salvation Army was established in Slough some ten years earlier.

Members of the 3rd Slough Boys' Brigade pose for a photograph to commemorate their winning the Battalion Drill Competition, the Squad Drill Cup and Battalion Gym trophy in July 1950. Captain Soloman is in the front row, fourth from the left.

The 2nd Slough Troop. A solemn group of scouts and cubs pose for a photograph.

On your marks... Off! The Grapes public house is the start of this early twentieth-century race.

Hospital Sunday Parade, c. 1920. With banners flying, the procession makes its way along William Street towards Crown Corner. Lynes' shop was a confectioners in 1920, but four years later C. Lynes was at the North Star Tavern.

Hospital Parade. Although this parade along Albert Street has not been positively identified, the inclusion of band, horses and carts, caravans and a fire engine suggests an important occasion for the community. Hospital parades were for fun and fund raising.

Chalvey Stabmonk procession, late 1930s. The Stabmonk ceremonies, which ostensibly commemorate the death of an organ grinder's monkey, are intricately woven into Chalvey folklore, and are a focus for community identity. The processions were revived in the 1930s when the banner was designed by the Chalvey 'mayor'. It depicts the four local industries – taking in washing, making babies, drinking beer, and working in the local 'treacle mines'!

A Royal Visit, 6 April 1962. Crowds cheer Queen Elizabeth as she drives through Slough on her way to visit Slough College.

Opening the mentally handicapped children's workshop in Elliman's Avenue in February 1963. The Queen Mother and one of the instructors watch a young girl operate her machine with intense concentration.

A marathon race, 1908. The race began at Windsor Castle; here the runners are seen in Slough High Street.

A superb gift. Horlick's presented an ambulance to the St John Ambulance Brigade in the 1930s. The ceremony took place in the grounds in front of the factory.

SOUTH BUCKS ELECTION, 1900.

GOOD GOVERNMENT & NATIONAL PROSPERITY

Registered Design.

THE FAVOUR OF YOUR VOTE AND INTEREST IS SOLICITED BY

The South Bucks election, 1900. W. Grenfell lived at Taplow Court and stood as the Conservative candidate for South Buckinghamshire which in 1900 included Slough. He was the successful candidate. It was his first as a Conservative: until his opposition to Gladstone's policy of Home Rule for Ireland he had been a Liberal.

COMPARISONS.

Mr. Gladstone's Government, 1894.	Lord Salisbury's Government, 1899.
Exports and Imports total £624,000,000,	£749,736,161
Seven per Cent. Unemployed.	Two per Cent. Unemployed.

13,774,990 more tons of Coal raised in 1899 than in 1894.

14,000 fewer able-bodied paupers in 1899 than in 1894.

£40,398,500 more in Savings' Banks in 1899 than in 1894.

1,614,740 more Savings' Bank accounts in 1899 than in 1894.

Between 1896 and 1900 there have been built and building—
25 Battleships, 44 Cruisers, 58 Torpedo Boat Destroyers, 8 Sloops, and 2 Gunboats. Total 137 Vessels.

Secure continued Prosperity in Trade

AND

Poll Early for GRENFELL,

THE POPULAR CANDIDATE & WORKING MAN'S FRIEND.

Nine

Yesteryear's Shopping

'Shopaholics', supermarkets and 'retail therapy' are terms which belong to the shopping revolution of the last few decades. But there have been many more changes since 1900 – the replacement of family businesses by national chain stores, the appearance of mass-produced goods, self-service, 'muzak' and the packaging of almost every item. Shop opening hours have also changed. Half-day and lunchtime closing are things of the past, but late-night shopping has come full circle since the beginning of the twentieth century. At that date, however, shop assistants were expected to work a twelve-hour day and clean the shop!

A High Street saddler, *c.* 1910. Leather goods of every kind are advertised on the shop wall or displayed for all to see.

Lidstone's shops in the High Street, *c.* 1920. The original shop at 154 High Street was opened in the 1880s. Within a few years the house next door had been acquired for a corn chandler. It was rebuilt twice after fires and at one time included a purpose-built restaurant seating 100 people.

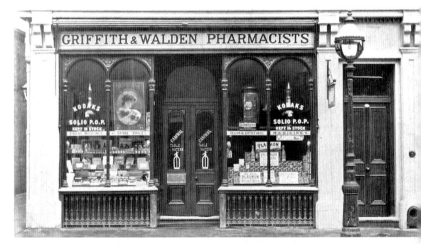

Richard Griffith was established in Slough by 1851 with a chemist's shop at Buckingham Place. It seems likely that Griffith & Walden became the twentieth-century successors – but at no. 71 on the other side of the High Street.

The High Street looking west from Crown Corner, 1928. 'Motor Works' seems a grand title for what was a repair shop and petrol station. Notice the kerbside petrol pumps and the slogan 'Motorists Wise Simoniz'. The shop was there for over seventy years.

Wadley's Motor and Cycle Garage, c. 1920. In 1911 the business was advertised as cycle maker and repairer at 206 High Street. By the date of the photograph Wadley's had taken over the adjacent house and expanded to become a garage. But why was there a railway signal post in the forecourt?

Left: Fuller's Store at Slough, *c.* 1905. This retail outlet for the brewery was next door to the Grapes beerhouse. Fuller's Brewery still operates at Chiswick but no longer with the names Smith and Turner.

Below: Harding's butchers shop, early twentieth century. It was commonplace to see meat hung outside such shops. Their advertisement shows that Hardings had a royal warrant and the royal arms are clearly visible above the shop. This was the first shop in Slough to have a telephone. Today the site is occupied by W.H. Smith.

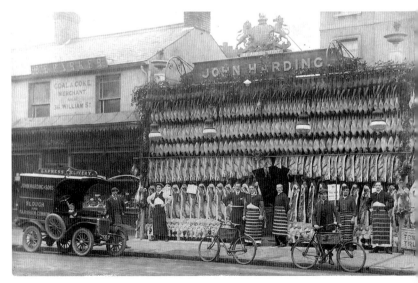

House advertisements. Many small businesses had advertisements painted on their houses, like Simmons in Stoke Road (c. 1911) and Bowyer's in Mackenzie Street, who were builders and decorators.

DIY the old way. Rabbitt's were established in Slough for more than sixty years; there you could buy according to your requirements, not according to the size of the pre-packaged merchandise. Rabbitt's had more than one shop in Slough.

Gordon Burgess, the co-author's father, was in business at 10 Chandos Street as a hairdresser from 1930 to 1964. The Macdonald Permanent Waving system advertised in the window involved a contraption placed over the customer's head which used steam to 'cook' the curls. One can only marvel at the discomfort women had to endure to enhance their appearance!

A delivery van, before 1914. At this date Thomas Grace's tobacconists shop was at 168 High Street. The driver is Miss M. White of Abbey Farm, Burnham; she was an aunt of Peter Ballinger, to whom this book is dedicated.

Thomas Grace, tobacconist. By the date of this photograph, taken sometime before 1920, the firm had moved further down the street, almost to the corner of Chandos Street. The public house on the right is the Golden Eagle.

Left: A striking display. Who would not be impelled to stop and look at this window of Lipton's shop in the High Street? Grocers and provisions merchants needed to do everything possible to attract customers as there were then ten other competing shops in the High Street.

Below: A Slough Co-op shop. This establishment is thought to be at Upton Lea. Great effort has been made with the window displays.

Slough Farm Dairy. The history of Slough Farm can be traced back to the early years of the seventeenth century, its farmhouse being within the village of Slough.

Bloxsomes, corn and coal merchants of Windsor Road, c. 1915. By the late 1920s the firm had premises in the High Street and owned malt houses in Alpha Street.

The Little Zoo pet shop, 1959. This aptly named pet shop opened in the 1930s in Chandos Street. The shopkeeper, John Dollery, is seen with a great crested cockatoo on his arm, talking to Peter Aust. This cockatoo could usually be seen in his cage on the pavement and heard talking to the passers by. Notice the advertisements for Spratt's dog food; they are found in quite a number of photographs of shops.

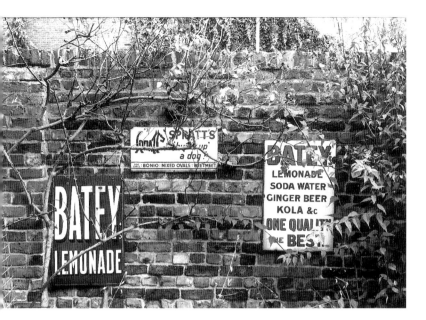

Above: Metal advertisements surviving in a Slough garden. Neither Batey's or Spratt's are local products, but advertisements for them were commonplace in the area.

Right: Reward cards for good school attendance. Scott's, the firm which issued this card, one of a series of six, had premises at Slough.

REWARD CARD.

Presented to.....................

With the Compliments of the Proprietors of
Scott's Emulsion.
SLOUGH.   *See back.*

Gathering in the harvest. According to this advertisement for Hadfield's corn manure,
Mr Robert Lee of Slough testified that he had the best crop of wheat for twenty years when
he used the manure for the first time. But who was Robert Lee? Although Robert Lee is said
to be 'of Slough', in the 1940s he was farming near Stoke Poges Common.

Wonderful manure! Miss Stevenson of Colley Hill Farm also could not speak too highly of the
product. 'The crop stood up with stiff straw and well corned'. The farm is also to the north of
Stoke Poges.

Right: Elliman's Embrocation advertisements. James Elliman began manufacturing his famous product about 1847 behind his draper's shop in the High Street. The factory was built in Chandos Street in the 1870s. It continued in production until 1961 when Elliman's was acquired by Horlick's.

Below: A selection of ginger beer bottles from Slough bottling factories and a brewery.

HORLICKS LIMITED
SLOUGH, BUCKS.

MILK STORAGE

CEREAL STORE

IN THE PAN ROOM

FILLING & PACKING ROOM

A postcard advertisement for Horlick's factory. In 1906, James Horlick chose to build his malted milk factory at Slough in 'ideal country surroundings', but with the advantage of easy access to the railway. The distinctive design of the factory soon became recognized nationwide.

Right: A display of Horlick's products. The business was sold to Beecham's in 1969, but it still trades under the name of Horlick's and one can still enjoy the malted milk drink which made the firm famous.

Below: A tea lady at Horlick's during the Second World War.

Junction of Mackenzie Street and the High Street, early twentieth century. One of the best-remembered shop windows in the High Street was that of Headington's. The intricate patterns made with the different grains were a perennial fascination to young children. The shop was opened in 1910.

...ngton's to Richard Bentley of The Mere. The Headington family also ... Court Farm as well as managing business premises at the corner of

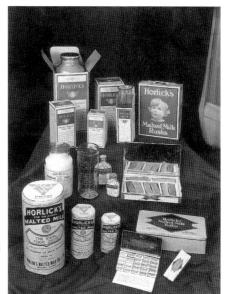

Right: A display of Horlick's products. The business was sold to Beecham's in 1969, but it still trades under the name of Horlick's and one can still enjoy the malted milk drink which made the firm famous.

Below: A tea lady at Horlick's during the Second World War.

Junction of Mackenzie Street and the High Street, early twentieth century. One of the best-remembered shop windows in the High Street was that of Headington's. The intricate patterns made with the different grains were a perennial fascination to young children. The shop was opened in 1910.

A receipt from Headington's to Richard Bentley of The Mere. The Headington family also farmed Cippenham Court Farm as well as managing business premises at the corner of Mackenzie Street.